Come, Let's Praise the Lord!

By Mary Curtis Lucas

Copyright © 2004 Mary Curtis Lucas

All rights reserved. No part of this publication may be reproduced, stored in a retrieval system or transmitted in any form or by any means electronic, mechanical, photocopying, recording or otherwise, without the prior written permission of the publisher.

Published by:

Poetry of Today Publishing
2073 Stanford Village Drive
Antioch, Tennessee 37013-4450
www.poetryoftoday.com

Book Cover Design by:

Kasie Shaw

Library of Congress Catalog Number: 0-9755554-1-3

International Standard Book Number (ISBN):
0-9755554-1-3

SAN: 2 5 4 - 5 5 5 1

Printed in the United States of America

If you purchased this book without a cover, you should be aware that this book is stolen property. It is reported as "unsold and destroyed" to the publisher and neither the author nor publisher has received any payment for this "stripped book."

Introduction

I have been a person who likes to try many things! Things may fall by the wayside as I start a new project. These poems seemed to have come into my head without any effort on my part. I do believe they are from my Heavenly Father. I praise Him for this opportunity to share them with you. In that I am 63 years old, this shows me you are never too old to try something new. If God leads, then I must follow. May your journey through this book encourage, uplift and inspire you. I pray that you are drawn closer to our Lord and Savior, Jesus Christ.

Mary Curtis Lucas
2004
Because of Calvary

Dedication

First of all I want to honor our friends Ray and Adrien Durham for their faith in Christ as Ray suffered and lost the battle with cancer this year. My first poem was to their Family. Now the verses just keep flowing.

The next is my precious Mother who had ten children, of whom I am, number ten. My Mom was a true lover of poetry. I don't remember her having time to write any herself. Now she and Daddy are with the Lord. I still miss them. I am so glad that I know I will see them in Heaven. Then there are my wonderful Pastors and Christian friends at Calvary Baptist Church in West Branch, Michigan who have helped me see that this book is a good thing to pursue.

Last but not least is my new friend and writer Diane Chamberlain who has encouraged me to keep writing. Diane Chamberlain is the author of "You Are Not Alone In A Lonely World".

I praise the Lord for this wonderful opportunity He has given me to share with others.

Mary Curtis Lucas
2004
Because of Calvary

Encouragement

For those who need lifting up or need a laugh, read on. May these poems lift you up and give you a chuckle.

As I reread them and remembered the wonderful times with family and friends, I just get so filled with joy.

May these words help you understand the Word of our Lord, and how He loves all of us. Live for Him, and we will see all of you in Heaven someday.

I praise God that He has chosen me to serve you by sharing what He has given me. May God bless you as you live for Him!

Mary Curtis Lucas
2004
Because of Calvary

Table of Contents

Introduction	3
Dedication	4
Encouragement	5
Come, Let's Praise The Lord	9
Alive Forever	10
At The Foot of The Cross	11
Baby Dedication	12
Be Not Afraid	13
Be Ye Salt	14
Blessed Be	15
Calvary	16
Chosen Few	17
Come And Share	18
Country Fun	19
Cousins	20
Come Watch and Pray	22
Creation	24
Crossing Jordan	25
Daddy	26
Doctor's Day	28
Faith	29
Family Times	30
Fear and Praise	31
Finishing Well	32
Five P's of Peter	33
Follow Me	34
From My Heart	35
Fruit of the Spirit	36
Go	37
God Is In Control	39
Good Morning Father	40
Grandkids	41
Happy Adversity	42
He Arose	44
Hear My Prayer	45
Heart Conditions	46
Hosanna	47
Jesus	48

Keep Me Lord	49
Look Around	50
May I Be A Servant	51
Mission Trip	52
Mother	53
Music	54
Motorcycle Papa	55
My Flower Garden	57
My Garden Gala	58
My Husband, My Friend	59
My Mate	60
My Pain, His Pain	61
My Prayer	62
Names of God	63
New Life	64
Old Folks at Home	65
Quilts	66
"R" Rated	67
Rewards	68
Salvation	69
Seasons of Life	70
Service Men	71
Seven Rules for Our Lives	72
Sewing	73
Shop Till I Drop	75
Sisters	76
Surrender	77
Talents	78
Thank You	79
Thank You for My Children	80
Thank You for the Roses	81
The Arrival	82
The Beauty of the Rainbow	83
The Old Man	84
Then Comes the Spring	85
Today	86
Trumpet	88
Trust	89
What Is Life?	90
Where Can I Sit?	91

What's In A Name	92
Who Killed Jesus?	94
Winter Days	96
Winter	97
Wisdom	98
As You Finish	99

Come, Let's Praise The Lord

Come with me and praise the Lord
Let's join our hearts in one accord.
Lifting up to Him our praise
That will last throughout our days.
Giving all the glory to Him
Our lights will not grow dim.
Singing, with voices high
We'll be singing until we die.
All our lives to surrender,
We need never wonder,
Where we will spend eternity
For in Heaven we will be.

Alive Forever

Alive forever how could it be;
That Jesus Christ would die for me.
He on the cross was crucified
For me that day He gladly died.
As punishment for my sin;
I want to cast my all on Him.
Father I thank You for Your Son,
That day, Heaven for me was won.
One day eternally I'll live,
Because Your Son You did give.
The pain You felt within Your heart
As the veil was rent apart!
This was the way You choose I see,
From sin's power we were set free.
Up in Heaven soon at His feet,
It is the place that we will meet.
Thank You Father again I say,
I'm so glad You're not far away.

At The Foot of The Cross

Today, please stand with me
At the foot of Calvary's cross,
Look with me at Jesus
He paid all my sin's cost.
The empty cross is a symbol,
Of the Savior who hung there,
His blood was shed for mankind
For Jesus truly cares.
He cares that we don't have to
Bare our own sin's price,
He was the sinless one
He was the perfect sacrifice.
He isn't on the cross today
For He ascended into Heaven;
The Father took Him from the grave
For us He has arisen.
Alive forever more is Christ
The one who paid for my sin,
By receiving Him as Savior
To Heaven you can go with Him.
My Savior, alive and waiting
To be my friend and guide;
Is always near beside me
And with Him I will abide.

Baby Dedication

It's time to dedicate my child
Unto the Lord above;
To thank Him for this blessing
He has given us with love.
My child was given by the Lord
For me to hold today;
I gladly give him back to You
To serve You and obey.
With friends and family here today
Please pray for us to live,
As parents serving Christ always
To Him our children freely give.
Help us to teach them in the Word
Your servants to obey;
That as they grow in wisdom
They will follow You always.
To nurture and admonish them
For this we gladly do,
May Jesus Christ be seen in them
Because they followed You!
We want our children to do God's will
Be sensitive to His voice
May Jesus Christ be seen in them
Serving God as their first choice.
To You Lord we do surrender
This child you've given us,
If missionary, pastor, servant be
It is in Your love we trust.

Be Not Afraid

I ask myself why do I fear
What man may do to me?
I forget that my Master
Has truly set me free.
I feel so inadequate
And secretly I worry,
I want to do things myself
And get the answers in a hurry.
I try to handle things myself
I shouldn't ask the Father,
It is just a small thing
He hasn't time to bother.
The anxiety will soon pass
I'll make it through someway,
How foolish I am, you see
Why didn't I just pray?
My Heavenly Father You are rest
I need to come to You
Help me not be so foolish
For You always see me through.
Your arms are held open wide
Waiting for me to come,
To the place of perfect rest
In the place that I call home.
Heavens gates swing open wide
Waiting for the Bride,
May we bring many with us
As with You we will abide.

Be Ye Salt

The salt of the earth are we
But please don't lose your savor,
Salt then is good for nothing
No good to our Savior!
If then it is thrown out and trampled
Under the feet of men;
So let your light shine on
And make it bright again.
A city that is on a hill
It cannot hidden be,
Or lamp under a basket
It is no use to Thee.
Put it on the lamp stand
So it can light the day,
Let your light shine for Jesus
Pointing others to the way.

Blessed Be

Blessed be the poor in spirit,
For theirs is the Kingdom of Heaven.
Blessed are the ones that mourn,
For comfort is to them given.
Blessed are the meek
For the earth they seek,
If for righteousness you thirst,
You will be filled first.
Blessed are the merciful
For mercy they obtain.
Blessed are the pure in heart,
They with God will reign.
Peacemakers are so blessed,
For they shall be called Sons of God,
Those persecuted for righteousness,
Theirs is the Kingdom of the Lord.
Blessed are you when persecuted
And evil falsely said against you,
Rejoice and be glad in the Lord
Your reward in Heaven is true.

Calvary

In my pain I would cry
There Jesus would hold me fast;
Until pain eased and I could pray
He held me 'til it passed.
He was always there beside me
No need to wonder why,
This time of pain was mine to bare
My Jesus was always nigh.
I think of the pain He suffered
There on Calvary's cross,
He asked for God to help Him
As His life's blood for me was lost.
I want to thank You Father
That You suffered there for me;
I cried for You while You hung alone
Upon the cross of Calvary!

Chosen Few

Today I heard the message
Of God's chosen few;
They are the Jewish peoples
I had forgotten what I knew.
The Master came to save them
The Gentiles He loves too,
He is the Messiah Lord and King
I share it now with you.
Jesus shed His blood on Calvary
That from sin we be set free;
Spear and nails and crown of thorns
He bore for your and me.
His death, burial, and resurrection
It is very plain to see,
He is waiting in Heaven today
To welcome us for eternity!
He is the great Messiah
The one and only King;
Receive Him as your Savior
And let the joy bells ring.

Come And Share

Come to salvation now
Do it without delay,
Surrender to His blessed will
Receive Him and obey.
Be diligent in the Word
Grow to live and obey,
Joy you will have forever
Please don't stay away.
Baptism is the next command
Into the waters go;
Death, burial, and resurrection
Your testimony to other's show.
Now go to the world
Share what you have found,
That they may know Jesus too
And show His love around.

Country Fun

When I was a teen at home
I was the youngest of ten
There never was a dull moment
Life was very eventful then.
I remember times of fun and games
Baseball, football, and hide and seek;
Taffy pulls and hayrides
We had fun every week.
Neighbor kids, and all of us
There were so many friends,
We knew that on any one of them
We truly could depend.
We rode to Sunday school together
The youth meetings were so neat,
We got together in our homes
Our studies were complete.
The missionary led our Bible Study
From God's Word so true,
He taught us the importance
Of serving God in all we do.
I thank God for His servants
Who willingly gave their all;
We found out Jesus
Could be our all in all.

Cousins

The cousins came to our house
To spend a week with us;
We had six of them
We could have used a bus.
Two vehicles we needed
To travel very far;
We went to special places
In the truck and in the car.
One day Ray took us on the pontoon
On it we gently did glide,
We caught fish, just minnows
With Gramps by our side!
There on the lake we saw a loon
Her babies with her came
And in the tree we saw an eagle
And loved it just the same.
We had picnics in the park
What fun we had together,
The sun was very hot
But, we loved it no matter.
Then the boys built a campfire
The hot dogs we did roast,
Then came the s'mores we made
Of those we ate the most.
What fun they all had
As they played badminton;
Grandma set on the porch
Playing with the kitten.
We can't forget the trip we made
As we ate pizza there at G's
Who had the best, I would guess
The one with the most cheese!

Cousins
(Cont'd)

To Macdonald's and Dairy Queen
We enjoyed it all so well
What do you think, should all of this
To our parent's we should tell?
We can't forget the buffalo
What big old things they were,
We stayed far away from them
They were covered with ugly fur.
Remember how hot it was
Gram sprayed us with the hose,
But, I wished she hadn't sprayed it
Up everybody's nose.
In the woods we did walk
And sometimes we did run,
It was great on Grandpa's farm
We cousins, we had fun.
Next door there were goats
Boy, were they such fun,
They would chase after us
When from them we would run.
Then when we had went home
Grandma quietly said,
"I think the time has come
For me to go to bed!"

Come Watch and Pray

Jesus to Gethsemane came
Asking His disciples to watch and pray,
His body was sorrowful and asked
Could you pray with me today?
Oh my Father if it could be
Let today this cup pass,
I asked not my will be done
For on you my life I cast.
When He came to Peter, he was asleep
Not watching with Him there,
Just one hour is all He asked
To watch, to pray, to care!
The spirit is so willing
The flesh it is so weak,
I am so sorry Jesus
I just fell asleep.
The third time Jesus found them
He said, my friends sleep on,
The hour is come upon me
When the betraying has begun.
Judas came with the multitudes
With many clubs and swords;
He betrayed our Blessed Savior
Our precious King and Lord!
A kiss was all it took from one
To show he betrayed the Lord;
One of them with Jesus
Took up his trusty sword.
Off came the ear of one nearby
But Jesus touched the man,
His body became whole you see
Jesus healed once again.

Come Watch and Pray
(Cont'd)

Jesus willingly was led away
His cross to gladly bear;
His prayer was not my will be done
For Father I know you are there.
To do my Fathers will I come
That men might from sin be set free;
This is the will of my Father
This is His will for me.
My prayer today is to be living
A committed life for You;
May Jesus Christ be seen in me
And faithful in all I do.

Creation

Do you believe the story?
That the earth just begun;
Into place it all fell
And then it was all done?
Look, how perfect are the seas
The sky and earth so vast;
This took a Creator
To make it all to last.
The rivers all run full and free
The mountains all so high;
The grass grows so rich green
Just watch the clouds go by.
See the birds they are so many
The animals they are too,
But the Creator made even more,
He made me and you.
Many trees to hold the birds
And make for them a home,
The flower's bloom in beauty
Everywhere you may roam.
Then mankind He created
This was to worship the Father,
Come now and bow down
Don't go any farther.
Serve the God who made the world
And the world to come;
Take Him as your Savior and
Heaven will be your new home.

Crossing Jordan

Our church has a quartet
If you haven't heard them yet,
You must hear Crossing Jordan
Sometimes they need a warden.
Joel keeps the men in line
In harmonies they tell,
Of their precious Jesus
They sing so very well.
We listen to Joel and Eric
Then come Jim and Bill,
We never get enough music
For our hearts to fill.
They sing of Amazing Grace
And of Excuses too,
Praising God above
In everything they do.
Thank You God for voices
Willing to sing Your praise,
May they follow Jesus
For all their living days.

Daddy

I didn't know my Daddy well
When I was a wee tot.
I knew he worked so hard to feed
His family, were a lot.
Our family was so very many
Ten to be exact there were,
It took so long to count us all
But, he knew that we were there.
Were there to work the farm as he
Was splitting stone for homes, so concise,
Mom taught us all how to catch
The friendly farm cat and mice.
As we did farming Dad built homes
We all had things to do;
There was some time for mischief though
For fun we loved through and through.
I remember once a week
My Dad would do his shave,
I was the first in line to get
My kiss if I behaved.
Some times the strap his razor used
Was placed on my behind,
Could it be from sassing back?
Or did him I not mind?
One time I remember
I sassed my Mother back,
Dad was standing very near
And I got a nasty, deserved slap.
Mom preferred to use the switch
It hung over the kitchen door,
I think I was the first in line
For I deserved it more.

Daddy
(Cont'd)

Why don't we learn from listening?
It seems we want our way,
But, what we get, we deserve
The piper we have to pay.

Doctor's Day

Hurry to the doctor
Your appointment is at two,
Now you sit and wait awhile
There's patients' ahead of you.
It's only three and I'm in a room
Soon now I will get to see,
The doctor or nurse will come
By four, I hope this will be.
Everything is doing fine
You are healthy as can be
I'll just put you on some pills
Until you again I see.
Are they pills for sugar
Or are they pills for cure;
If nothing is wrong with me
I don't need them, that's for sure.
I will see you another time
To make sure you are okay,
The bill is all I need to see
To cure me right away!

Faith

I find access to my Father
Through the communion of prayer;
I am so blessed to know Lord
That you are always there!
I come in faith believing
That the Word of God is true,
I thank You for the Bible
I love it through and through.
You give my life much purpose
To others I must share,
You will save them from their sin
For You are the one who cares.
We must have unity in worship
To praise Your name today;
We sing and lift our voices
And live for You always.
Yielding to Your spirit
Now I choose to live,
Committed to Your will God
Is the best that I can give!

Family Times

Our family gets together
It is on Christmas day,
What a great time we all have
No one could stay away.
We laugh and play together
We eat a lot we do,
It takes us a long time
As we partake of the fondue.
Everybody smiled for me
As great pictures we got,
Who's making funny faces?
Man, was that an awful shot.
Uncle Tom, you have to smile
That ugly face can't be,
We know you are better looking
That much we can see.
Thank you Father for the gift
Of Your Son so rich and free;
My prayer for this family
Is that they always live for Thee.

Fear and Praise

Oh, magnify the Lord today
His name exalted be;
Let's praise His name together
Let's praise Him you and me.
Let's look to Him with faces bright
Aglow with love for Him;
Be not ashamed, for Christ we love
Let not our light grow dim.
The angels of the Lord encamped
Their presence ever near,
When in Jesus we do trust
We never need to fear.
Oh, fear the Lord
Ye, saints of His;
Lift up your hearts
And with Him live.
Oh, taste and see His goodness true
For you He died you see,
Blessed is the man who trusts
My God in only thee!
Come, ye Children of the Lord
Listen please to only me,
And I will teach you the fear of God
If you will follow my example free.
Who is he, who desires life,
And loveth many ways;
That he may see only good
Then follow Jesus today!
Depart from evil, and do good
Seek peace within thy breast,
To follow and pursue it
And receive perfect rest.

Finishing Well

I started out so small and free
Just a tiny tot;
I saw, as I grew older
I could learn a lot.
My personality was encouraged
To be seen and used;
Some people laughed at me
And really were amused.
Sin's nature could be seen
As I grew and watched others;
It had to be corrected
When I copied from my brothers.
When I gave my life to Jesus
The Bible became my guide,
I kept my eyes toward Him
For He was by my side.
The great example He became
An taught the way to give;
And now I'm telling others
Jesus is the way to live.
God, my great desire
Is that I would finish well;
When I leave this world behind
My testimony friends will tell.
Faithful to the end
That is my heartfelt plea,
Bringing others with me
Because Jesus they see in me.

Five P's of Peter

I thank God for His presence
As beside me He does walk,
When I feel so alone,
With Him I can freely talk.
God has the power to overcome
All sin for me effaced,
Jesus took them all from me
My sins He did erase.
All my provisions He supplies
My needs are always met,
How could I not praise Him?
How could I ere forget?
The purpose Jesus has for me
Is to serve Him evermore,
To share His love with others
That Him they will adore.
What a promise I do have
Heaven will be mine,
When I have Jesus as my Lord
His promise is divine.

Follow Me

My child ponder this my Word
Unto My voice take heed
Keep them in your heart today
And I will supply your need.
Let them not from Your eyes depart
And ever close upon Your heart,
May your heart with diligence be
For out of these issues, follow me.
Put away a crooked mouth
And evil lips from you,
Let your eyes look right on
And your eyelids look straight too.
Ponder the path of your feet
May they established be;
Turn not neither left nor right
Have your feet follow me.
This my child, will lead you home
With Jesus to abide;
Until the day we meet in Heaven
He'll be right by my side.

From My Heart

From my heart I thank You
Father for Your love,
You are precious to me
I know You are above.
Thank You for filling
All my needs today;
May I never from You
Choose to go astray.
Such peace I have within my breast
As only You can give,
I choose this day and always
For You to ever live.
When one set of footprints
I can only see,
I know at this moment
You are holding me.
Many times I stumble
I fall unto my knees,
That is when You hold me close
And You listen to my plea.
Such mercy and such grace
You give me every day,
May I never, ever
From You turn away.
How unworthy I am today
But I thank You for the price,
That You paid on Calvary
What a complete sacrifice!
So I thank You once again
That You are in my heart,
May I share with others?
That will be my part.

Fruit of the Spirit

The fruit of the Spirit is
Love, joy, and peace;
I know they are written
Especially for me!
Long suffering, kindness, and goodness
Must apply to my life.
God has shown them to me
By His great sacrifice!
Be faithful and show goodness
Then self-control will follow,
We must remember
That the way is very narrow!
If in the spirit we do live
Then in the spirit walk.
Serve the Savior always
And with others let us talk.
Bare one another's burden
And fulfill the law of Christ,
Serve and love Him always
To have eternal life!

Go

When the Lord says go
I must obey His voice,
My desire is to always
Make His will my choice.
I want to do my best for Him
To follow all the way;
I want the peace that Jesus gives
If I do, what His words say.
My way is always present
My heart can ever stray,
But my greatest desire is
To follow and obey.
Obey my Father and to serve
Please Lord, help me do;
For when this life is over
I will come to You.
Heaven will be wonderful
To kneel at my Savior's feet;
I want to love and worship Him
Till this life is complete.
With all the angels I will sing
With voices raising to the Lord;
All Saints voices are ringing
Our hearts in one accord!
I know You will be with us
On that bright and glorious day;
As we kneel and praise Him
And worship Him always.
There's joy in serving Jesus
It makes our life complete,
There is nothing better
Than to worship at Jesus feet!

Go
(Cont'd)

At the feet of Jesus
Is where I long to stay,
Down on my knees in worship
From Him I shall not stray.
I long to be more like my Master
To serve Him is my goal,
So I must let Him lead me
And then come forth as gold.

God Is In Control

Today I read of David
In the precious book so true
His heart was filled with living
What God would have him do!
He came to conquer Saul the king
But God bid him let Saul go.
David took the spear away
And this let King Saul know.
Our God is in control
Of all He bid's us do,
So King Saul turned to God that day
For David had been true.
May we follow in the steps of Jesus,
May our lives show Jesus love,
For with this our love for others
We lead someone to Heaven above.
Heaven will be beautiful
So share this news with all,
Be sure to follow Jesus
And answer His every call.
As we listen to God's voice
As we hear His word;
Our hearts will be softened
To know that others heard.
They heard of Jesus' saving grace
They see the joy He gives,
What wonderful blessings we receive
As for Jesus we do live.

Good Morning Father

I thank You for the night of rest,
May today I do my very best,
To others Your love I show,
That in Your mercy they may grow.
I want to walk right by Your side,
That in Your love may I abide.
May my life show forth Your love!
To lead others, up above.
Your Word this day shall lead the way
That faithfully I always stay.
So living, sharing the Gospel true;
That others Jesus may see You.
No greater service could I do
Than leading other's unto You.
Such love my precious Savior gave,
The blood was so I could be saved.
Thank You for the joy You give,
As for my Savior I can live.
May my family live for You!
In everything they say and do.
I give to You my everything,
As joyfully I praise and sing.
I shout Your praises with my voice,
And make Your precious will my choice.
I love You Jesus

Grandkids

Grandkids are the greatest
What smiles they can give,
It makes my life worth living
The joy for me to live!
We love to talk on the phone
And hear of all their fun,
We know they are very busy
And always on the run!
Some are in the country
Some are in the town,
If you get to the camp
The others there are found.
Lord I thank You for the kids
Their smiles melt my heart,
My prayer for every one is
That from You they never depart.
May they find mates who love You too!
And serve You joyfully with praise,
And follow You where ere You lead
And are blessed by Your great grace.

Happy Adversity

It looks like my spelling is off
But it is plain to see,
There's one who leads us through
Each step of adversity!
We may have adverse trials
We may suffer great loss,
Remember joy comes in sorrow
For Jesus was on the cross.
Trials come to make us strong
And on God's arm we lean,
He's there beside us all the way
And helps our heart stay clean.
Life's burdens aren't to break us
They're just to make us strong,
We may bend from time to time
But, with Jesus we can't go wrong.
When trials and temptations come
Just kneel to God in prayer,
You'll find Him not far away
For He is always waiting there.
Let's choose to have joy in trials
For patience we will win,
A closer walk with Jesus
Is where it all will end!
If any of us lack wisdom
There's a place we can find,
The source where all our needs are met
In His great love sublime!

Happy Adversity
(Cont'd)

Let no man say when he is tempted
God did this to me,
Satan is the tempter
So we must turn and flee.
Flee to the arms of Jesus
He's waiting for you there,
Just open your arms to Him
And give Him all your care.

He Arose

H- Hallelujah Christ has risen!
E- Ever making intercession.

A- Alive in heaven He is today;
R- Risen there and going to stay.
O- One and only Son of God;
S- Sinless One that earth did trod.
E- Eternally with Him we'll live.

If our lives to Him we give.

Hear My Prayer

Hear my prayer when I call
Christ enlarge my heart
To listen when You speak
And from You not depart.
The Lord hath set apart for Him
The godly who don't deserve;
I know Him as my Savior
And it's Him I want to serve.
I stand in awe of His great love
His blessings I receive,
I praise Him for His saving grace
That Him I might not deceive.
Offer the sacrifices of righteousness
And put your trust in Him,
Then we'll share the good He does
And let not our light grow dim.
May Your light of countenance glow
Upon my life today;
That the brightness of Jesus
Be seen in me always.
Gladness in my heart You give
More than the wine increase!
I will lie down in the peace You give
My sleep it will not cease.

Heart Conditions

Over forty, have a bad heart
It is never too late to start.
Exercise and lose some weight.
Hurry now, it's not too late.
Has your heart the Father met,
Come now let's get set.
To the Lord you must give,
Your heart to Him, so you can live.
Exercise your heart with prayer
Give Him all your love and care.
Give to Him all your worry,
Do it now, please do hurry.
Read the Word what joy He gives,
When for Him you faithfully live.
This is the best exercise,
For you Heaven is the prize.

Hosanna

The Son of God came riding
Into town on a colt;
Setting on his back
The donkey didn't even bolt.
The multitude laid garments
And palms upon the ground;
This here is the Master
The one they had found.
Many man, did mock Him
Are you really the Son of Man?
Hosanna to the Son of David;
They repeated once again.
This is Jesus the children cried
Hosanna to the Son;
We will gladly worship Him
His work will soon be done.
He came to die on Calvary
To pay my sins for me,
By shedding His precious blood
That I from sin would be set free!
Oh the pain of the cross
He suffered there I know;
By receiving Him as Savior
To Heaven I will go.
Life eternally is mine
By bowing at His feet,
Come along with me and
Jesus you will meet.

Jesus

I slept
Jesus wept.
He died
I Cried.
He bled
And shed
His blood
For me!
He chose
He arose.
I confess
He does
The rest!
He lives
I give
My life
To live
For Him!
He'll come
I'll go
With Him
Ever more
To Abide.
Praise Him
Love Him
Serve Him
Ever more.

Keep Me Lord

Father You are to me
My rock and fortress true.
Deliver me, oh my God
That I see only You!
For You are my hope today
May my mouth be
With it honor You always
So others see Your face in me.
In my old age keep me fast
While life here on earth be;
Faithfully living out my life
To please only Thee!
Now with old age my hair is gray
Forsake me not I pray
Give strength to those who follow
And Thy power of praise today!

Look Around

Did you see the grape clusters
And see how the seeds do grow,
Or do you look at them and say
They are full of seeds you know?
The rose has a fragrance
The sweetness of perfume;
Did you know that there are
Many a thorn among the bloom!
How about the soda pop
On the hottest day;
It is almost empty now
It's only full half way?
Let's not think negative
Look on the bright side,
Our hearts need to be full
To in God's love abide.
Look to the Father
He will fill your cup,
Just lift your joys to Jesus
And He will fill you up.

May I Be A Servant

Jesus came to the disciples
He knelt, their feet to wash;
Then dried them with the towel
To get a point across!
I know you washed your bodies
Before you came to me,
But your feet are soiled
You have traveled far you see.
One of you today
Is not clean of heart,
When the washings over
From me you will depart.
One of you will betray me
For just a little silver;
Oh! could you forsake me?
I pray that it would be never.
Am I willing to be a servant
To follow in the Master's way,
May I be willing to serve like Him
And help others along the way?
May today I serve my family
And serve my neighbors too,
Dear precious Heavenly Father
I would be more like You?
May the pedestal's we are on
Be tumbled to the ground,
So the love of Jesus shines
And everywhere abound.
I choose to kneel at Your feet
To be humbled by Your love;
That Your servant I will be
Till we meet in Heaven up above.

Mission Trip

Our daughter left for Africa
On a Mission trip,
Flying for twenty three hours
Was quicker than a ship.
They went into the desert
To the Muslim tribe;
To share the Word of God
That for them Jesus died.
The story of the one lost sheep
That Jesus went to rescue,
Was done in flannel graph
So they can be saved too.
Oh that many may find Christ
It's why they went to tell,
Salvation's plan to others
For we know it all so well.
Of the Christ that gave His life
His blood on Calvary;
May they accept it gladly
That from sin they be set free!

Mother

Today I think of my Mother
She went to be with You,
Behind she left the love of God
By living for Jesus true.
She taught us how to love
No matter what the task,
We need to love one another
That's the thing that will last.
We were taught to help our neighbor
Even if we had not much to give,
To share with those in need was best
The way Jesus would have us live.
There is joy in serving others
With sharing what we receive;
It goes so much, much, further
And helps others to believe.
By sharing things like Jesus love
Will help our neighbors know
That if we surrender to Jesus
To heaven we too will go.
Mom, even though I miss you much
Because of what you taught,
I know one day in Heaven
It will not be for naught.
Together we'll praise Jesus
And sing on Heavens shore,
We'll glory in His presence
And have peace for evermore.

Music

Hark, I hear the birds singing
They are praising the Creator,
A choir to their Maker be
Their voice's never greater.
They fly up to our feeder
And share with one another,
It doesn't matter that
All are a different color.
The woodpecker's very large
And eats side by side,
With the little nuthatch
They take it all in stride.
May we, like the birds
Get along so well,
And the love of Jesus
May we to others tell?

Motorcycle Papa

Our Papa has a Harley D
Can you believe it's so?
On the back is Grandma
As down the road they go.
Gram's hanging onto Papa
Afraid to trust it all;
But, just look at Papa smiling
He's having quite a ball.
See the bugs on Papa's teeth
They say it means what joy,
Gram says it's a second childhood
He's just a little boy.
We're on our way to our grandkids' house
Bring out the bread and butter,
As on the road again we go
Our hearts are all a flutter.
I've been with Papa many years
Forty-two to be assured;
I hope we make it many more
As soon as Papa's cured!
This problem that he has
Comes from Harley fever,
I guess this is what retirement brings
It makes you young forever.
Gram says she is too old!
To follow him behind;
But on the road we go again
As love is oh so blind!
There is an option for the seat
Papa suggests a sidecar,
But we know he'll pull the pin
And send her off afar.

Motorcycle Papa
(Cont'd)

When Papa gets tired of listening
The rev of engine roar,
I'm signing of the ear set now
While down the road we soar.
As we rise tomorrow
Upon the bike we go,
You'll never know which way we went
As we don't even know.
Together is important
As we travel off this day;
You'll know that we're together
And blessed along the way.

My Flower Garden

What joy it brings to me
To plant the flowers I sow,
They are so very pretty
When they begin to grow.
The colors they do vary
Blue, pink, yellow, and red;
They raise their petals upward
As from the sun they're fed.
The daffodils and tulips come
The first to lift their color;
Then come the lovely lilies
In beauty with one another!
My favorite is the lilac bush
The color is so blue,
The fragrance is so wonderful
The smell is ever true.
I love to add new flowers each year
So many God has made,
The beauty of the rose He gives
The colors never fade.
Jesus is the Rose of Sharon
The Bright and Morning Star;
I love to praise and worship Him
Even from afar.

My Garden Gala

Today we meet together
Many ladies in one accord;
The thing we would like today
Is to worship our precious Lord.
Lots of fun and crafts we do
We laugh and have such fun,
This is the joy of ladies day
And we don't have to run.
We meet new friends and old alike
We let our hair fall down,
This gives us a break from stress
We never need wear a frown.
Laugh, smile, and crack your face
It doesn't even matter,
If you hear something fall
Just laugh and let it clatter.
Friend, this your day of gala
This is your garden party,
Just set back and have some fun
It doesn't matter if you're tardy.
Hear a message, sing a song
If you mess up your craft;
It doesn't even matter
As long as you can laugh!

My Husband, My Friend

Jerry became my friend
Many years ago;
My friend became my husband
As to the altar we did go.
We pledged our love forever
That is a long, long time,
To be faithful to the end
He would always be mine.
The Lord gave us three children
We love them everyone,
First there came two daughters
Then God gave us our son.
We love our children greatly
So precious they are to us,
I'm so glad Jesus gave them
Even when they put up a fuss!
Now, we have grandchildren
Oh how we love them dear,
They are precious as can be
And we love to hold them near.
In our old age together
We spend much time alone,
Thinking of the days gone by
And wishing our kids to come home.
Come on home and visit
Let's set and talk awhile,
It's so wonderful to see
Everyone's great big smile!
Love grows greater
As in God's love we live,
May we share it with others
So they will also give.

My Mate

I thank God for my lifetime mate
To me he's been so good,
Sometimes things were hard
But Jesus understood.
There were times of plenty
And times of greatest need,
We had to watch our wants
To make sure it wasn't greed.
Our needs God did supply
He had the storehouse full,
He kept our hearts drawn close to Him
And things were never dull.
I well remember our neighbor Sam
He'd call for a hair cut,
God knew our every need
As Sam, gave me a buck.
The buck was for the milk that day
The kids had drunk it all,
Our needs the Father did supply
Before on Him we could call.
Thank You Jesus once again
How much we praise Your name,
My prayer to You today
Is that our kids feel just the same!

My Pain, His Pain

In my pain when I would cry
Here Jesus would hold me fast
The pain would ease, then I could pray
He stayed 'till it would pass.
At my side He's always there
No need to worry or sigh,
This time of pain for me to bear
My Father was always nigh.
But, as I think of Jesus
And the pain He had to bear
On the Cross of Calvary
He suffered for me there
Thank You, oh my Father
For the salvation You made free,
Because I gave my heart to Jesus
With You, one day I'll be.

My Prayer

Father today may I be;
Faithfully living all for Thee.
May others round about me see
Only Jesus living through me!
May my life shine all around
That my Savior ever abound.
May the me be set aside
May I fully in Thee abide!
Oh, how much I forget
That I must always let,
You lead the way to Heavens gate,
I know Father I can't debate.
You are faithful ever true
I know the best that I can do,
Is listen to Your voice today
For me it is the only way.
May I lead some soul to You
That to Heaven they go too.
What rejoicing there will be
When our Jesus we do see.

Names of God

For unto us a child is born
The Son of God is given,
For us God gave His only Son
So we could be forgiven!
Great names of my Master
Wonderful, Counselor, Mighty God is He,
He is human and Divine
Everlasting Father, Prince of Peace!
Personally today we can know Him
And embrace His great love,
In miracles and wonders
We can be with Him above.
His kingdom and His throne
Established it will be,
With justice and with judgment
Bring peace for you and me.

New Life

Today I saw a robin
It is the sign of Spring,
I now see the truth of it
For I just heard it sing.
The thrill of Spring to me
Is seeing things come anew,
This comes from our Savior
Who died for me and you.
The flowers will soon be blooming
The colors of many hue,
This too comes from Jesus
As only He can do.
The daffodils oh, so yellow
The tulips do their thing,
This could only happen
Because He is Lord and King.
The grass is really green
We will soon be mowing,
Thank You Lord for new life,
May I too be growing.
True life comes from God above
He gives to us so free,
He offers us salvation too
He gives it to you and me.

Old Folks at Home

Today I went to the old folk's home
Our Missionary Group goes to sing,
I came away being so blessed
I heard the joy bells ring.
Jack was one of the patients
He sang with joy, you bet,
So Jack and I lifted up our voices
And we sang a duet.
We sang how Jesus Loves Me
The others were so happy,
Then they joined their voices too
Those people are so snappy.
Smiles they give that lift your heart
They gave praise to our Savior true
The old folks are so precious and dear
I love them, I really do.
Thank you Father for time with them
As someday I will be,
One of the old folks there
Please send someone to sing for me.

Quilts

There are quilts of many colors
Red, green, yellow and blue;
Put them all together right
They bring out the best of you.
The pieces are so many
Put together just right,
And when you have finished
It is a beautiful sight.
With love you make the many squares
The shapes they may vary,
When you give it to a friend
It makes their heart so merry.
Our life is like a patchwork
With Jesus as the Maker;
If we let Him fit the pieces
We'll please our great Creator.

"R" Rated

"R" is for rejection
That our Jesus knew,
When He died on Calvary
For the sins of me and you.
We are so rebellious
That redeemed we need to be,
The Savior is the only one
Who could pay the fee?
Reconciled we need to be
To Jesus here today,
For He's the only one
Who can wash our sins away!
We need this blessed relationship
Please don't refuse,
Come today and accept
The blessed truth so true!
The results will be Heaven
With Him is the reward,
To live in Heaven forever
To live in one accord!
We will be received by the Ruler
The Wonder of My Soul,
Come unto Him now
Let Him take control.
Now, you've been redeemed by the Master
Righteous for eternity,
Into the Glory of the Lord
Come along and reign with me.

Rewards

For length of life and long days
His peace He will add to thee
Let mercy and truth not forsake
This is the best for me.
Bind them on your neck and heart
Follow Christ always,
Write them on your heart
And follow Christ today!
Understanding will be seen
By God and man alike;
Tell others of Jesus love
To Him they'll make their flight.
Trust in the Lord with your heart
All of it give to your Master;
Lean not on your own understanding
Depart from evil faster.
In all your ways acknowledge Him
And He shall direct your path
Be not wise in your own eyes
What's done for Christ will last!
Depart from all evil
And do well today,
Put Satan behind you
Do it now without delay.
This is health to the navel
And morrow to the bone;
This will take us to Heaven
A time to worship Jesus alone!

Salvation

S - Savior Lord and King
A - Always there for me;
L - Loving and forgiving
V - Very God is He.
A - Alive in Heaven today
T - There He waits for all.
I - Interested in all I do
O - Only listening for my call!
N - Never will He leave me
He's my all in all.

Seasons of Life

In the Spring of our lives
So fresh and free are we,
As older we become
We begin to see.
That Summer is not far away
As we start to grow older;
We can see more clearly now
And we get a little bolder.
Fall is on its way
How much more we see now;
Life is moving faster
I can't believe it, wow!
Now it's Winter
Life has passed so fast,
Now I see it clearly
Life is almost past.
From the cradle to the grave
Time has flown from me,
I know Jesus as my Savior
Soon with Him I will be.

Service Men

As I look out my window
There is an old elm tree,
On it is a yellow ribbon
It's there to remind me.
Of the men who are at war
My freedom they will win,
Lord I thank You for them
When will war ever end?
My brothers all were in the service
One was in Old Germany,
Two were in Pearl Harbor
Making it safe, for you and me.
One in Okinawa
One in Korea too;
God brought them safely home
I thank you God, I do.
The last was in 'the Reserves'
Here at home was he,
O praise God for protection
As He brought them all home you see.
Mama said, "It was the prayers"
She sent to God above,
For the protection of
Her sons she dearly loved.
I pray today as Mama did
So many years ago,
That You bring our men home soon
And cancel all the woe.
Comfort all those who grieve
Some men have gone on,
To meet the Lord up above
And some have come on home.

Seven Rules for Our Lives

What in life do you want most?
Is it fortune and fame?
For me it's taking my family with me
When it's Heaven that I gain.
What is the thing most on your mind?
Is it having money fare?
Or would you be content to
Meet your Savior in the air?
How is my free time spent?
Does it my Jesus please?
Does it please others too?
Or does it please only me?
Do I use my money?
To see the church increase,
Or do I give a few coins
So all the questions cease.
Does the company we enjoy
Bring honor to the Master?
Or, is it used to make others
Think I can live much faster?
Who do I look up to?
Whom do I adore?
Is it the Lord of Heaven?
Or, who ever comes in the door?
When I laugh is it because
Of someone's nasty joke?
Do I laugh with everyone?
Or, walk away provoked?

Sewing

Sewing was my first love
No pattern did I have
Just use a newspaper, Mom said
And it won't turn out too bad.
So from the time that I was twelve
My clothes I made a lot,
They didn't look very bad
So, many clothes I got.
I wore them to school
People thought them fine,
Momma said, "They look nice."
So I didn't even mind.
Practice does make better
The projects never ceased,
I made a special flower girl dress
I made it for my niece.
I made this for my wedding
And it was plain to see,
The dress it was so beautiful
And she looked just like me.
In later years my taste did change
And quilting I really enjoyed;
So off to 'Button Hole' I went
Where there, I was employed.
My home looks like a fabric shop
The first quarter I must get,
From every bolt of fabric
For quilting I must be set.
Our children all have quilt's today
To all of them I've given,

Sewing
(Cont'd)

So when I leave this world behind
Apart of me I'm leaving.
Thank you Lord for all You gave
For eyes, and mind so free;
Now I've went on to try
Writing a little poetry.

Shop Till I Drop

Here I am at Wal-Mart
Waiting for Ashlee and Kim,
So many people passing by
I just smile at them and grin.
Outside it is kind of misty
But in here it is hot,
I hope the drear of the rain
Doesn't cause me to spend a lot.
Here I sit with coke in hand
It gives to me some zip,
I'll just sit here and enjoy
While I take another sip.
Here comes a big man in just now
Two donuts in his hand;
Should I have one myself?
No, for me there is a ban.
I love to sit and watch the crowd
It takes up lots of time.
I really do enjoy it much,
As it fills my heart with rhyme.
Now my shopping's over
I've spent quite a bit,
Soon I'll be in the car
Oh boy! Now I can sit.

Sisters

God has blessed me very much
He has given me three sisters,
Everyone of them love the Lord
And all are faithful listeners.
I'm sure that we did have some spats
When we were very young;
But, as we older grew
We all new it was in fun.
Now in Jesus I have many sisters
Because of Christ you see,
We have wonderful fellowship
As in Jesus we believe.
The Holy Bible is our guide
Of our loving Savior tell,
In His Word He leads us
From the place called hell.
He tells of the Heaven above
Of streets of purest gold;
To it we will be going
We in His arms, He will hold.
Come along and be my friend
Come to Jesus too,
He is the greatest friend of all
For He is ever true.

Surrender

There have been times of many tears,
As I traveled through the years.
As unto Jesus I commit,
And on my knees I do submit.
How hard it is to surrendered be;
I like to have control of me.
How better life is today;
For letting Jesus have His way.
Why is it so hard for me to say
Lord Jesus please have Your way.
In the way my life is lived,
To You it all I gladly give.
May my family for You be,
A reflection of Your light in me!
I pray an example of You may show,
That in surrender they may grow.
One day before my Savior stand;
Until then please Lord take my hand.
And lead me to my home above,
Because my heart is filled with love!

Talents

Father forgive me
For the talents I didn't see,
My eyes were not open to
The things You gave to me.
I gladly give them back to You
No matter what the task,
I know what I do for You
Are the only things that last!
I give my voice to sing Your praise
To lift it up in song;
May my voice give You honor
To You I belong.
It seems You've given me poetry
The verses come to my brain,
May each verse I write
Be only for Your gain.
May they encourage others
To You Father would they go
We'll rejoice in heaven one day
Because we love You so!
May I come along side others
That to Jesus we will bring;
May the victory be Yours
As Your praise we will sing.
'Till we come to meet You Father
In the Heavens up above;
I'll praise and worship You forever
And share with others Your great love.

Thank You

God I thank You for the roses
The fragrance is so sweet,
I know someday in Heaven
My Savior I will meet.
At the feet of Jesus
I bow my heart to thee,
To ever praise and adore
Your servant I will be.
May Your will be my choice
For me to live is You,
That I may show others Lord
That they may serve You too!

Thank You for My Children

Lord, I thank You for my children
They mean so much to me.
That is why we gladly
Gave them back to thee.
Thank You for their smiles
The joy that they have been;
I praise You now for saving
Them from the path of sin!
Thanks for giving Christian mates
As lives they live for You,
They've led their children now
So they all know You too.
When this world we depart
And some of us must leave,
We'll know Jesus will comfort then
And we'll not have to grieve.
Yes, we will miss the ones gone home
That had to go ahead,
They will be waiting for us
Just as Jesus Christ has said.
For up in heaven we will meet
In a great reunion there;
There will be no more sorrow
There will be no more care.

Thank You for the Roses

Dear Lord I want to thank You
For the roses that You give;
The fragrance is so beautiful
It gives me joy to live.
I must remember with the roses
There also comes the prick,
The sharpness of the thorns I feel
Which can make my heart grow sick.
The sickness can be of the heart
If your blessings I don't receive;
When I forget to follow You
And let my soul to grieve.
Take time to smell the roses
As you go along life's way;
Your happiness will overflow
And show others Jesus today.
There's joy in serving our great God
Who gives us eyes to see
The loveliness of the roses bloom
To follow You eternally!

The Arrival

They just delivered Papa's Harley
He's grinning from ear to ear,
I guess this is for real
And I need to trust, not fear.
It is so big and heavy
But a beauty it really is,
So soon he'll be on the highway
As down the road he'll whiz.
Joining friends and having fun
Bikers we will soon be,
We'll have on our leathers
You won't believe it's me.
I don't believe I truly think
That on this bike I will ride;
I hope my body does hold up
Especially my backside!

The Beauty of the Rainbow

Have your seen the rainbow
With it colors of great hue,
In it God has promised us
That He will be ever true.
The promise to never send a flood
To cover the earth surface;
Because of His love for us
We would do Him service.
To love and praise Him for His love
For heaven can be obtained,
Nothing will be lost to us
It will all be for gain.
If to Him we give our lives
To live for Him today;
We'll be in heaven with Him
If we pray and obey!
Share the promise of the bow
With others you do meet,
We will see the Master
And worship at His feet.

The Old Man

To walk in vanity of mind
Is not to please the Lord,
We must increase in His likeness
And be of one accord.
Having the understanding of darkness
Alienates us from His grace,
We must turn our hearts to Jesus
And look into His face.
Don't live a life of uncleanness
Don't follow Satan's way,
Just turn your life over to the Master
And follow Him today.
Put off the former thing of sin
To Jesus you submit,
He'll give you joy in living
When to Him you commit.
Be ye angry, and sin not
The sun go not down on your wrath;
Let all communication there
On your Savior to be cast.
Be ye kind one to another
Tenderhearted, forgiving, then see,
The love of Jesus leads His children
To be gentle kind and free.
Be therefore, follower's of Christ
As dear children we can live,
Sacrifices and offerings
Of sweet savor we will give.
Redeeming the time
Because of evil days;
Look up to the Savior
And give Him all your praise.

Then Comes the Spring

Today came the first robin
He's hopping all around,
The snow has almost vanished
You can really see the ground.
Spring is around the corner
The flowers soon will bloom,
Up from the earth they're peeping
Their appearance will still the gloom.
Oh the beauty of the Spring
The freshness of the air;
Look around and you will see
Our Jesus is everywhere.
Only God can make a flower
It's beauty in full bloom,
His promise of life to come
New life is coming soon.
With the Spring comes the rain
The freshness pure and clean;
The flowers receive new life
As from earth's sun to glean.
Today my heart is overflowing
For the beauty of the day;
May I show love to others
So they love You always!

Today

May this day my joy show forth
To others it be shown,
That they may see Jesus love
May it everywhere abound!
With joy may happiness come in
And others follow my Lord,
May Christ only be seen in me
And we are all one accord.
Today I read in His word
How everyone is loved;
By our precious Savior
Who is watching from above!
He's there to give us our desires
If we ask in Jesus name;
He knows our needs before we ask
And gives to us the same.
Our needs He joyfully supplies
Our wants we may not need,
He looks them over with His love
And throws out all the weeds.
So many weeds in my garden heart
I give them all to Him,
With tender care He cleanses me
And gives me the best of them.
Come to the Savior on bended knee
Confess your heart and care;
At the foot of the cross
He will meet you there.
He knows your heavy burdens
He knows the joys you share,
He knows your disappointments
How very much He cares.

Today
(Cont'd)

Let's follow in His footsteps
He'll lead us all the way,
Until we get to heaven
On earth we need to stay.
Serve Him with our very best
This joy to others share,
The praise will come in serving
Our Jesus without any care!

Trumpet

Davey let your trumpet sound
Let it be heard all around.
Let it sound forth with love
To our Savior up above!
Thank you for serving God,
With your horn and with your love.
We praise Jesus with you too,
We love music through and through.
Sound the trumpet and sing a song
To our Jesus we belong.
One day the trumpet of God will sound,
Then in heaven we'll be found.
Singing, praising, our precious Lord,
All the music in one accord!
Come on sound the trumpet again,
For together we will reign.

Trust

For length of days
And life so long;
You can have peace
When to Jesus you belong.
Let mercy and truth forsake thee not
Just bind your neck with them,
Write them on your heart today
And find favor with your friend.
Trust in the Lord with all your heart
Not on your own understanding lean;
In all your ways acknowledge Him
And He will your heart keep clean.
Be not wise in your own eyes
Fear the Lord and depart from evil;
This is the way to follow Christ
And separate from the devil.
It's health to thy navel
And marrow to thy bones;
Honor the Lord with your first fruits
Until the day God calls you home.
Thy barns shall be filled with plenty
Thy presses shall burst with new wine,
The day is soon appearing when
God calls us to come and dine.
The Lord chastens those He loves
Correction, don't be weary;
This is the way God shows His love
So don't be sad or dreary.

What Is Life?

"L" is for our loving Savior
Who died on Calvary
He gave up His life
To save a wretch like me!

"I" is for the innocence of Jesus
He had no sin at all,
His blood was shed for me
I must answer His call.

"F" is for forgiveness
That is offered to each man,
We can live forever
That is God's special plan.

"E" is for eternal life
You can have it for the taking,
It is free to everyone
If your sins you are forsaking.

Where Can I Sit?

There were the sons of Zebedee
Who wanted the seat of choice
Jesus told them the Father chooses
So listen closely to His voice.
Not on the left or right for you
Not ever could you win,
The Father makes the choice you see
And it shall be given then.
Whosoever is among the great
Shall your minister be
Whoever is the chief here
My servant He will see.
Even the Son of Man came not
To be ministered unto;
He came to minister and to give
His very best for me and you.
Jesus gave His life in ransom
His blood for me He gave,
This blood was spilled on Calvary
That my life might be saved!
I praise You Father for such love
I thank You with all my heart,
My prayer is that from this day forth
I will not from Your love depart.

What's In A Name

The name of Elohim is God
The strong and faithful one;
He gave to us the precious gift
He gave His only Son.
Jehovah God, we come to know
The self existent one;
He is God and Lord above
The one to whom we must come!
God wants us to experience
His power and glory true,
That His great love to others show
They can have Jesus too.
My El Shaddi He is All Sufficient
Mother's heart of God has He
Almighty God, Creator here
He knows what's best for me.
My Father He does comfort me
So others I can lead,
With unconditional love
From sin may be set free.
El Olam is everlasting
Forever He will be
I praise Him for His precious blood
He shed on Calvary.
I love the God, El Roi it is
The God who does see me;
The God of all comfort
That is what He is you see.
If we disobey Him
Uncomfortable we should be,
He's there to comfort and encourage

What's In A Name
(Cont'd)

God's there for you and me.
Jehovah is a special name
The self-existing one;
He is the great "I Am"
The joy of what's to come.
God cannot change, for He is God
The one in heaven stands
One day with our Savior
Heaven will be very grand.
Our God loves the sinner
For this you clearly see,
His love is there to lead us home
For all eternity.
Eternity with Jesus
What rejoicing for us there;
No sorrow, pain or suffering
Not ever any care.

Who Killed Jesus?

As I look at the cross
I wonder who killed God's Son,
Was is me that did it
Or was it another one?
As I look in God's word
It is plain to see
There are several answers
So listen close to me.
The guilty are the sinners
That includes us all,
Then the Jews and Romans
Into line did fall.
The Jews hung our precious Lord
On the cross of shame;
The nails in His hand's and feet
Jewish people are the one to blame.
The thorns placed on His head
The nails in His hands and feet;
Were placed on Him in anger
But it didn't mean defeat.
Then I see the Bible records
That God sent His Son to die,
On the cross of Calvary
For sinners such as you and I!
Now I see no one took His life
He gave it full and free,
To pay sin's final price
For sinners just like me.

Who Killed Jesus?
(Cont'd)

We all are guilty I can see
Receive His salvation free,
Then your life will be complete
To live with Him eternally!
Christ is alive in heaven
With arms opened up wide,
Waiting for us to come home
There to ever more abide.

Winter Days

Winter days in Michigan
Can truly be such fun!
As snow comes down and wind blows
You really need to run.
So beautiful the trees hang down
Their boughs so laden be;
With pure white snow upon them
They are drooping down to me.
God's wonderland is everywhere
As I sit and look around;
I thank Him for His blessings
As to me they do abound.
Out of my front window
The birds fly to and fro,
As the sun shines down upon them
It sets their world aglow.
May my life be white as snow!
Pure and clean for all to see;
That everyone around me
God, may they see only thee.

Winter

Winter is beautiful in Michigan
The snow looks almost blue,
It is a sight to behold
It thrills me through and through.
Be sure that you bundle up
When for a walk you go,
The sun is shining up above
But, in a minute it may snow.
The weather changes quickly
Be sure that you take care
A blizzard can come up fast
And you'll be caught unaware.
Satan to is like the weather
You never know when he'll appear,
So be very sure that you
Keep Jesus ever near.

Wisdom

Hear ye children the instruction
From your Father up above;
The same teachings you receive
From your earthly father with his love!
I as the Father's Son,
Tender beloved in sight,
He lead me to my Savior
Who is my heavenly light!
Wisdom is the leading lesson
Exalt her and promote,
She shall bring you honor
On hearts tablet it is wrote.
Follow not the path of the wicked
Avoid it ... pass it by,
If we follow mischief
We will have much need to cry.
Keep your heart with diligence,
For the issues it will show,
That with the things you will do
Jesus will help you grow.
Let your eyes look forward
Toward the prize to win;
Ponder the path your feet shall trod
And keep your life from sin.
Turn not to the right or left
Just press on to the Savior,
With Him out front to lead you
Be on your best behavior.
My son attend to wisdom
And bow your ear to discretion
This the way to perfect joy
And you have learned your lesson.

As You Finish

I truly pray you have enjoyed this book. It has been such a blessing writing these poems. I pray you get as much out of reading them as I have had in writing them. Who would have ever guessed that as of two months ago, that I had never written a poem? God has blessed me so much, being able to sit at my computer and write as if I were in my right mind! Oh what a blessed Savior we have.

I have had many surgeries in the past few years which has limited me in many ways. Now, God has given me poetry. Keep watching as I have many more poems on the way!

My life verse is Proverbs 3:5-6. Trust in the Lord with all thine heart and lean not unto thine own understanding. In all thy ways acknowledge Him and He will direct your path.

NOTES

NOTES

NOTES

NOTES

NOTES

NOTES

NOTES

NOTES

NOTES

NOTES

NOTES

NOTES

Poetry of Today Publishing

www.poetryoftoday.com

Poetry of Today Publishing
2073 Stanford Village Drive
Antioch, TN 37013-4450

Other Titles by Poetry of Today Publishing

If you would like to order other titles published by Poetry of Today Publishing, check the book(s) desired, complete the form below and mail it with your payment to the address provided. Our books make great gifts!

_____ My Life Is Like A Story - $8.00
_____ Every Eve - $8.00
_____ Thank God for Salvation - $8.00
_____ Reflections on Life - $8.00
_____ Lord's Tears - $10.00
_____ I Love Jesus Christ - $8.00
_____ Human Race Evaluate - $10.00
_____ The Heart Cries - $10.00
_____ You Are Not Alone In A Lonely World - $8.00
_____ Joy In The Morn' - $8.00
_____ Inner Living - $10.00
_____ Come, Let's Praise The Lord! - $10.00
_____ Fire In The Blood - $10.00
_____ Lift for Living - $10.00
_____ Women of the Bible: Their Stories in Verse - $10.00

Add $2.50 per book for shipping and handling for each book.

Name: _____
Address: _____
City/State: _____
Zip: _____

(Orders are shipped within five days of receipt.)